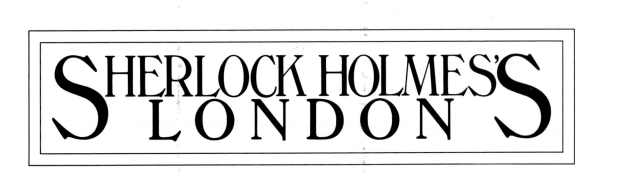

SHERLOCK HOLMES'S LONDON

SHERLOCK HOLMES'S LONDON

Following the Footsteps of London's Master Detective

Tsukasa Kobayashi

Akane Higashiyama

Masaharu Uemura

CHRONICLE BOOKS · SAN FRANCISCO

Acknowledgments

The editors would like to express their gratitude to the Trustees of the Wallace Collection, who permitted the reproduction of three of their paintings; to Mr. and Mrs. J. Hardcastle, who by special courtesy allowed us to take photographs in their pub "The Sherlock Holmes"; to Mr. J. W. Miller, who kindly allowed us to take pictures in St. Bartholomew's Hospital; and to Mr. and Mrs. Philip Buttinger, Esperantists who gave us many suggestions for our tour through the London of Sherlock Holmes.

First published in the United States 1986 by Chronicle Books

Copyright © 1984 by Tsukasa Kobayashi, Akane Higashiyama, and Masaharu Uemura. All rights reserved. No part of this book may be reproduced in any form without written permission from the publisher. First published in Japan by Kyuryudo Co. Ltd. 3–23 Kioi-cho, Chiyoda-ku, Tokyo, Japan 102.

Printed in Japan

Library of Congress Cataloging in Publication Data
Kobayashi, Tsukasa, 1929–
    Sherlock Holmes's London.

    Translation of: Shārokku Hōmuzu no Rondon.
    Bibliography: p.
    1. Holmes, Sherlock (Fictitious character)—Pictorial works.
2. Doyle, Arthur Conan, Sir, 1859–1930—Characters—
Sherlock Holmes—Pictorial works. 3. Doyle, Arthur Conan,
Sir, 1859–1930—Settings—Pictorial works. 4. London
(England)—Descriptions—1981–   —Views. 5. London
(England) in literature—Pictorial works. 6. Detectives in
literature—Pictorial works. I. Higashiyama, Akane, 1947–
    . II. Uemura, Masaharu, 1947–   . III. Title.
PR4624.K613 1986   823'.8   85-30895

ISBN 0-87701-380-2   10 9 8 7 6 5 4 3 2 1

Distributed in Canada by
Raincoast Books
112 East 3rd Ave.
Vancouver, B.C.
V5T 1C8

Chronicle Books
One Hallidie Plaza
San Francisco, CA 94102

CONTENTS

Map of London

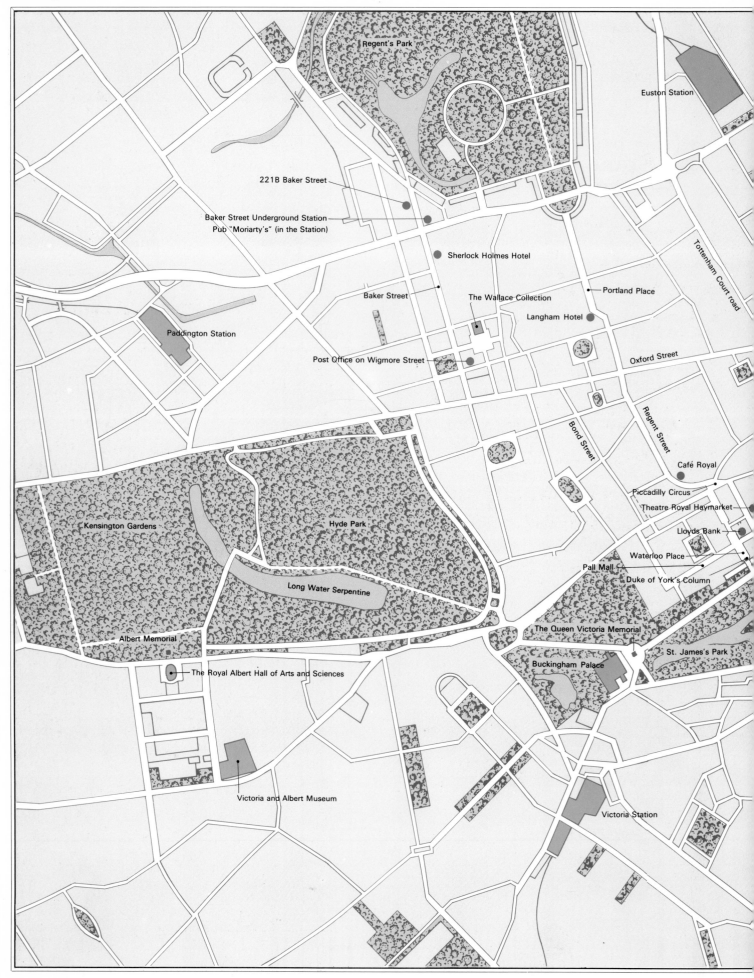

Regent's Park

Euston Station

221B Baker Street

Baker Street Underground Station
Pub "Moriarty's" (in the Station)

Sherlock Holmes Hotel

Tottenham Court road

Baker Street

The Wallace Collection

Portland Place

Langham Hotel

Paddington Station

Oxford Street

Post Office on Wigmore Street

Bond Street

Regent Street

Café Royal

Piccadilly Circus

Theatre Royal Haymarket

Kensington Gardens

Hyde Park

Lloyds Bank

Waterloo Place

Long Water Serpentine

Pall Mall

Duke of York's Column

The Queen Victoria Memorial

St. James's Park

Albert Memorial

Buckingham Palace

The Royal Albert Hall of Arts and Sciences

Victoria and Albert Museum

Victoria Station

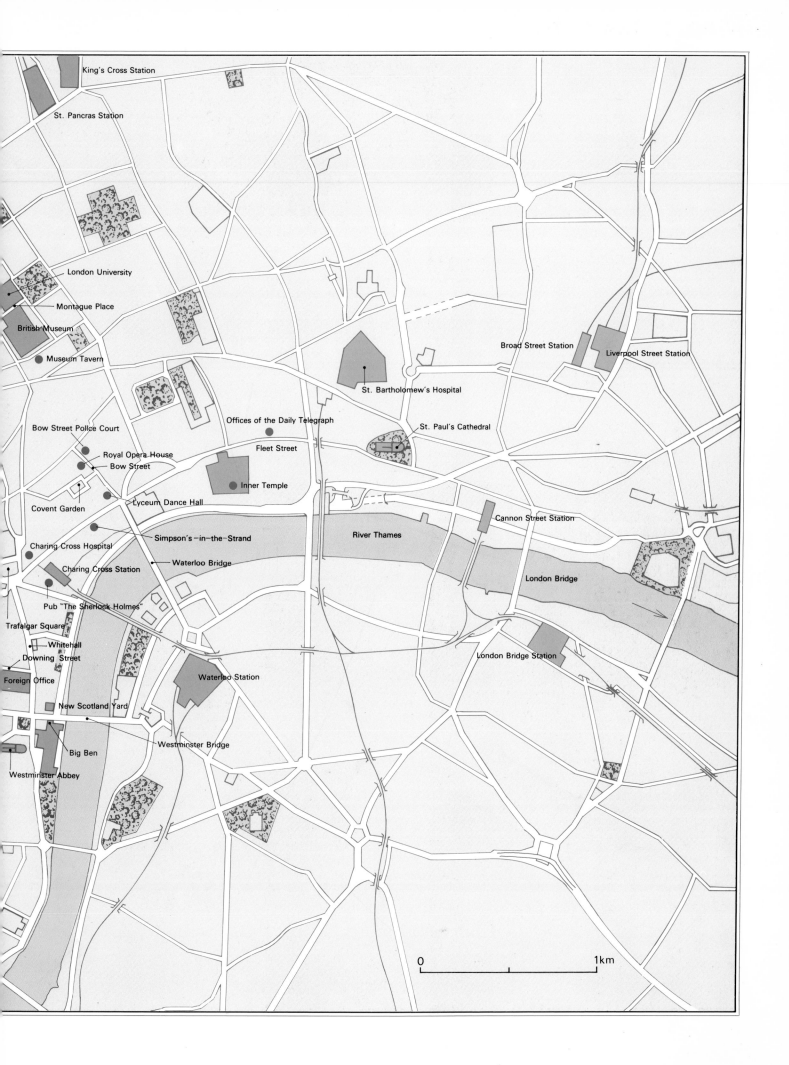

King's Cross Station

St. Pancras Station

London University

Montague Place

British Museum

Museum Tavern

Bow Street Police Court

Royal Opera House

Bow Street

Covent Garden

Lyceum Dance Hall

Charing Cross Hospital

Simpson's–in–the–Strand

Waterloo Bridge

Charing Cross Station

Pub "The Sherlock Holmes"

Trafalgar Square

Whitehall

Downing Street

Foreign Office

New Scotland Yard

Big Ben

Westminster Abbey

Westminster Bridge

Offices of the Daily Telegraph

Fleet Street

Inner Temple

St. Bartholomew's Hospital

St. Paul's Cathedral

Broad Street Station

Liverpool Street Station

Cannon Street Station

River Thames

London Bridge

London Bridge Station

Waterloo Station

0   1km

"I should like just to remember the order of the houses here. It is a hobby of mine to have an exact knowledge of London."
—————— *The Red-Headed League*——————

Sherlock Holmes

Portrait by Sidney Paget

Part I

LONDON
IN THE LATE
NINETEENTH CENTURY

Sherlock Holmes worked actively during the last quarter century of the Victorian era, when the British Empire was at the height of its prosperity. The radiant capital of this great empire was London. With the Industrial Revolution and the expansion of the railway system, urban communities developed tremendously, and England was transformed from a quiet, pastoral country into an industrial nation. During the Victorian era, the population of London leapt from 2 million to 6.5 million.

From the vast, world-wide network of colonies that inspired the saying, "The sun never sets on the British Empire," multitudes of people poured into London. The world's largest metropolis, London not only served as the centre of government, commerce, and industry, but also took the lead in cultural matters. Magnificent buildings and monuments lined its streets, and throngs of people and carriages jostled each other on the grand boulevards.

However, there was something besides the thick fog, stealing up on the flickering gaslights, that was casting a dark shadow on this lively metropolis. The increased urban population, the formation of a middle class, and the uneven concentration of wealth were causing a dangerous increase in crime. Thus, the stage was set for the appearance of *The Detective*.

London Bridge (ca. 1890)

Regent Street

*He quickened his pace until we had decreased the distance which
divided us by about half. Then, still keeping a hundred yards, we
followed into Oxford Street and so down Regent Street.*
——————*The Hound of the Baskervilles*——————

Piccadilly Circus

On the very day that I had come to this conclusion, I was standing at
the Criterion Bar, when someone tapped me on the shoulder, and
turning round I recognized young Stamford, who had been a dresser
under me at Barts.
——————*A Study in Scarlet*——————

Charing Cross Hotel (upper stories) and Charing Cross Station

I think I could show you the very paving-stone upon which I stood when my eyes fell upon the placard, and a pang of horror passed through my very soul. It was between the Grand Hotel and Charing Cross Station, where a one-legged newsvendor displayed his evening papers.

———— *The Illustrious Client*————

The Strand, looking east

Inner Temple

The Langham Hotel, seen from Portland Place

"In the year 1878 my father, who was senior captain of his regiment, obtained twelve months' leave and came home. He telegraphed to me from London that he had arrived all safe, and directed me to come down at once, giving the Langham Hotel as his address."
————*The Sign of Four*————

Bow Street Police Court

"Come this way, if you please." He led us down a passage, opened a barred door, passed down a winding stair, and brought us to a whitewashed corridor with a line of doors on each side. "The third on the right is his," said the inspector.
————*The Man with the Twisted Lip*————

St. James's Hall

He suddenly sprang out of his chair with the gesture of a man who
had made up his mind, and put his pipe down upon the mantlepiece.
"Sarasate plays at the St. James's Hall this afternoon," he remarked.
———— *The Red-Headed League*————

Royal Opera House (Covent Garden Theatre)

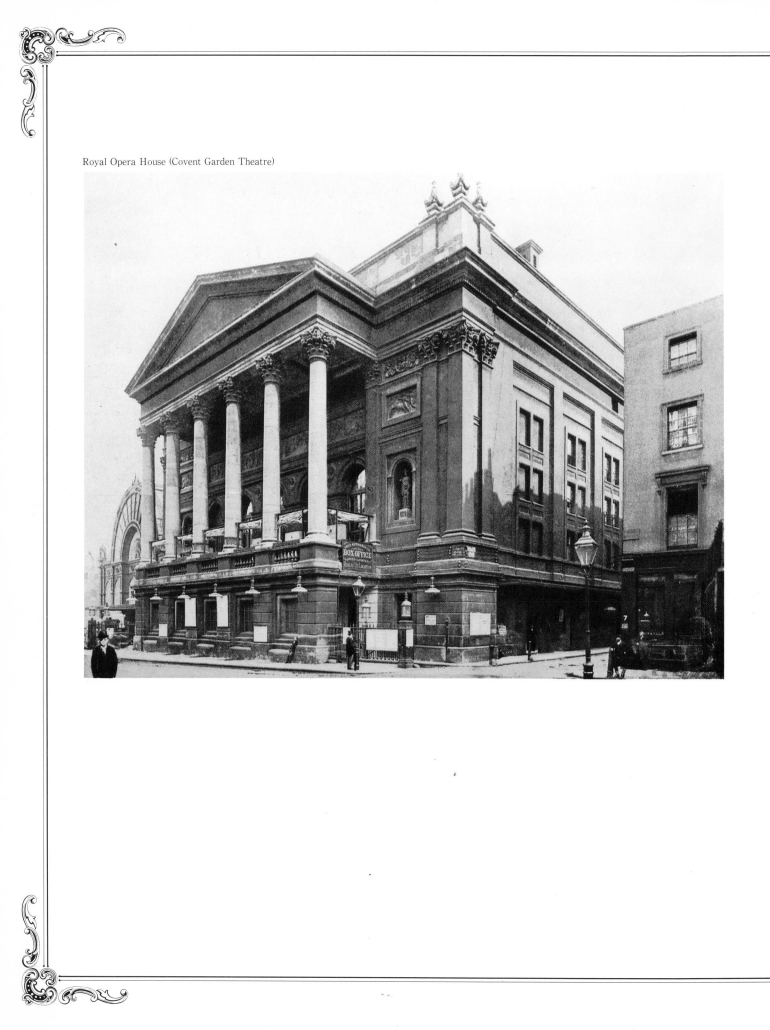

Theatre Royal Haymarket

"On that particular evening old Amberley, wishing to give his wife a treat, had taken two upper circle seats at the Haymarket Theatre. At the last moment she had complained of a headache and had refused to go."
——— *The Retired Colourman* ———

St. Bartholomew's Hospital (Bart's)−Henry VIII gateway

St. Bartholomew's Hospital−front entrance

St. Bartholomew's Hospital–courtyard

As he spoke, we turned down a narrow lane and passed through a small side-door, which opened into a wing of the great hospital. It was familiar ground to me, and I needed no guiding as we ascended the bleak stone staircase and made our way down the long corridor with its vista of whitewashed wall and dun-coloured doors.
————*A Study in Scarlet*————

The Thames and docks

While this conversation had been proceeding, we had been shooting the long series of bridges which span the Thames. As we passed the City the last rays of the sun were gilding the cross upon the summit of St. Paul's.
——————*The Sign of Four*——————

Looking southeast from Bow Church

STREETS

Sherlock Holmes was never at fault, however, and he muttered the names as the cab rattled through squares and in and out by tortuous by-streets. "Rochester Row," said he. "Now Vincent Square. Now we come out on the Vauxhall Bridge Road."

—————— *The Sign of Four*——————

❶ Holborn

❷ Northumberland Avenue

❸ Queen Victoria Street, with the offices of the Times

❹ Fleet Street

❺ Waterloo Place, with Duke of York's Column at right

❻ Newgate Street, with Newgate Prison at right

STATIONS

A brougham was waiting with a massive driver wrapped in a dark cloak, who, the instant that I had stepped in, whipped up the horse and rattled off to Victoria Station. On my alighting there he turned the carriage, and dashed away without so much as a look in my direction.

———The Final Problem———

Paddington Station

Paddington Station

STATIONS

Already the doors had all been shut and the whistle blown, when ——— "My dear Watson," said a voice,"you have not even condescended to say good morning." I turned in incontrollable astonishment. The aged ecclesiastic had turned his face towards me.

——— The Final Problem ———

❶❷ Euston Station
❸ St. Pancras Station
❹ St. Pancras Station, Midland Grand Hotel
❺❻ King's Cross Station

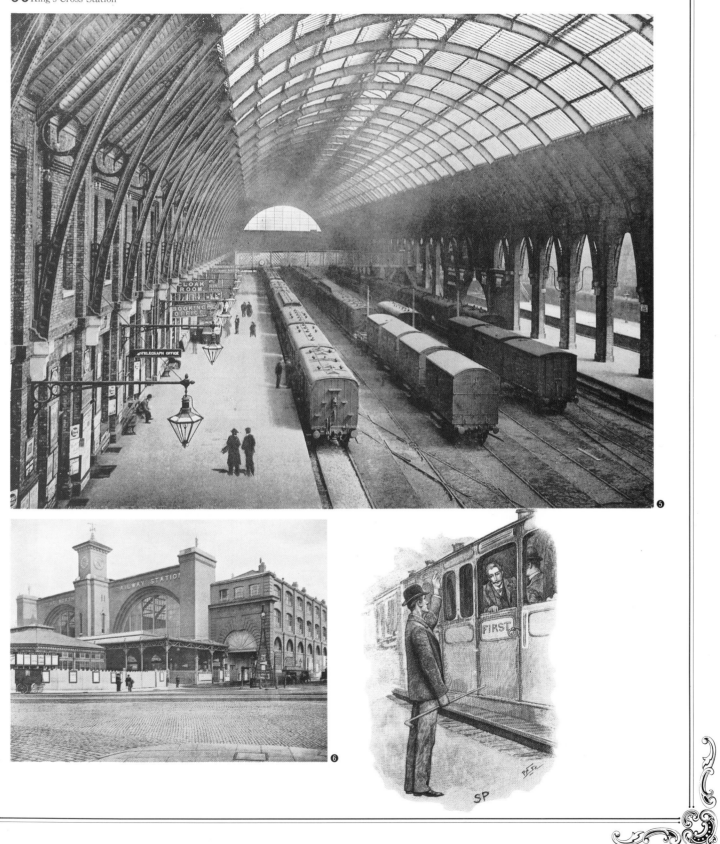

"Dr. Watson, Mr. Sherlock Holmes," said Stamford, introducing us.
———— A Study in Scarlet ————

Sherlock Holmes (right) was a famous consulting detective working in London from 1877 to 1903. Dr. Watson (left) was a medical doctor who lived with Holmes in the rooms at 221B Baker Street. He assisted the detective and recorded their adventures.

Part II

 **Pursuing the Footprints of Sherlock Holmes**

Baker Street (ca.1900)

Baker Street

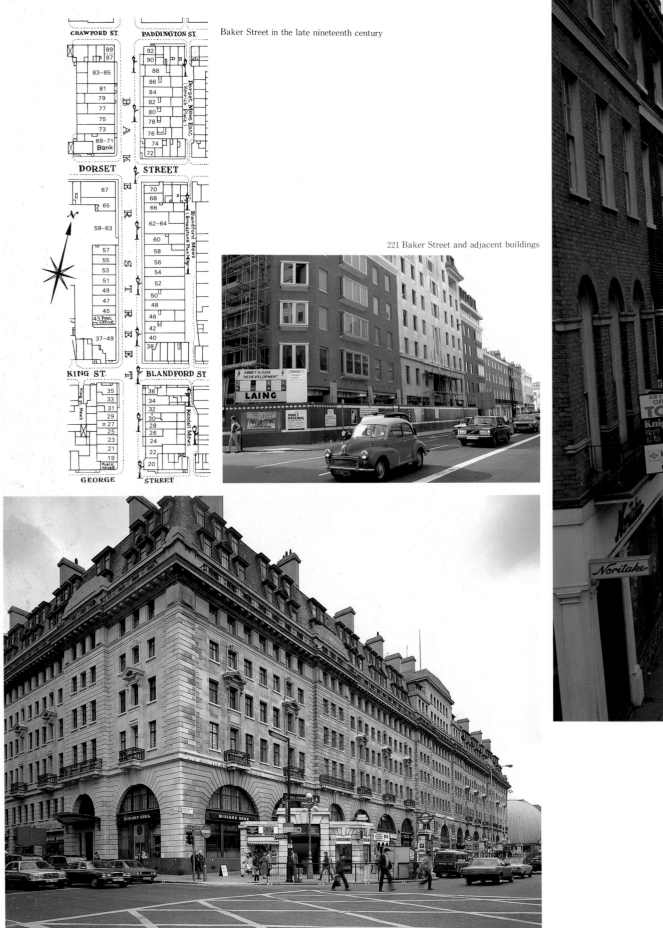

Baker Street in the late nineteenth century

221 Baker Street and adjacent buildings

Baker Street Station

View from the south

In the nineteenth century, Baker Street was situated at the far northwestern end of London. The city later expanded westward, so that one now sees it more as a large thoroughfare near the centre of the city. It has become a busy street, lined with shops and bustling with a never-ceasing flow of cars and people. At the time Holmes was renting his rooms there about a century ago, however, the area must have been much quieter. If one ventures into a back street, one discovers many old buildings still remaining that call to mind the Baker Street of old.

Baker Street
Underground Station

Baker Street Station is located on London's oldest Underground railway line, the Inner Circle. The walls of the station are steeped in history. There, remaining unchanged, are holes that must have let out smoke in an age when the trains still spewed smoke. Perhaps we can find Holmes's footprints there as well.

Illustrations on platform walls

The Hound of the Baskervilles

With long bounds the huge black creature was leaping down the track, following hard upon the footsteps of our friend. So paralysed were we by the apparition that we allowed him to pass before we had recovered our nerve.

The Speckled Band

Out from a clump of laurel bushes there darted what seemed to be a hideous and distorted child, who threw itself on the grass with writhing limbs, and then ran swiftly across the lawn into the darkness.

The Red-Headed League

Holmes fell upon his knees upon the floor, and, with the lantern and a magnifying lens, began to examine minutely the cracks between the stones. A few seconds sufficed to satisfy him, for he sprang to his feet again, and put his glass in his pocket.

The Sign of Four

The old man made a little run towards the door, but, as Athelney Jones put his broad back up against it, he recognized the uselessness of resistance.

The Solitary Cyclist

On the farther side of it, under the shadow of a mighty oak, there stood a singular group of three people. One was a woman, our client, drooping and faint, a handkerchief round her mouth.

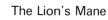

Charles Augustus Milverton

She had drawn a little gleaming revolver, and emptied barrel after barrel into Milverton's body, the muzzle within two feet of his shirt-front.

The Lion's Mane

The next instant he threw up his hands, and, with a terrible cry, fell upon his face. Stackhurst and I rushed forward — it may have been fifty yards — and turned him on his back.

Pub "Moriarty's" (in the Station)

Professor James Moriarty

"Elementary, Watson, elementary."

Professor Moriarty was the evil genius who was Holmes's rival. He was the Napoleon of crime. Although he is said to have controlled almost every possible sort of crime throughout London, this former mathematics professor has won a certain amount of popularity. This is no doubt because there is little feeling of reality to his crimes. Some people even hypothesize that Holmes and Moriarty were one and the same. His bold spirit of fair play is another reason why we cannot hate him entirely. There are, in fact, numerous pubs and restaurants that bear his name—what better evidence of his popularity!

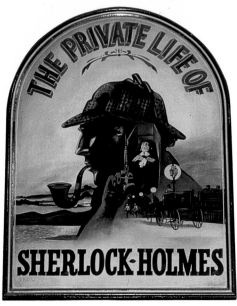

Sherlock Holmes Hotel

Front entrance (Chiltern Street)

Baker Street is said to have been laid out by William Baker in 1755. William Pitt, who became prime minister at the age of twenty-four and continued in that office for seventeen years, lived at No. 120, and Bulwer-Lytton, the statesman who also wrote popular novels, was born at No. 68. Another resident was Richard Burton, who was known for his exploration of India, Mecca, and Africa, as well as for his English translation of the *Thousand and One Nights*.

The deeds of these actual men, as great as they were, may fade from mind with time, but the name of Sherlock Holmes will live forever.

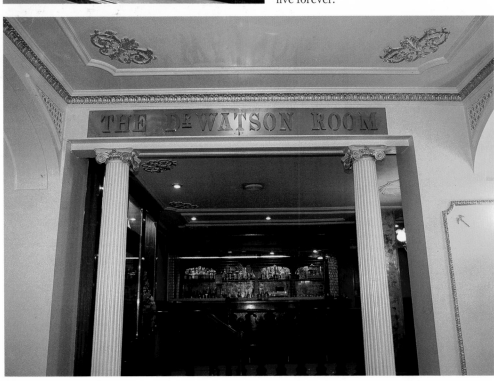

The Dr. Watson Room (Bar)

Baker Street entrance

The Wallace Collection

Holmes's artistic bent is attested to by his performances on the violin, his monograph on the Polyphonic Motets of Lassus, and his love of concerts. This aspect of his character no doubt has a lot to do with heredity, for he was a descendant of the French painter Vernet.

Holmes also appears to have been quite familiar with the works of Raphael Santi and Jean-Baptiste Greuze. Perhaps we should reconsider the previous assessments of Holmes that have tended to see only reason within him and should take into account his keen aesthetic sensibility as well. It is this sensibility that elevates his detective work from a science to an art.

Queen Victoria in Robes of State by T.Sully

A Storm with a Shipwreck by C. J. Vernet

Post Office on Wigmore Street

"It is fear, Mr. Holmes. It is terror." She raised her veil as she spoke, and we could see that she was indeed in a pitiable state of agitation, her face all drawn and grey, with restless, frightened eyes, like those of some hunted animal.
——— *The Speckled Band* ———

Not only the clients who visited him but even his fellow-lodger, Dr. Watson, were often astounded by Holmes's powers of deduction. In one case, his powers were put into action at a post office. His deductions, however, are such that, when the reasoning behind them is revealed, it seems anyone could come to the same conclusions simply by observing closely. Just like a magic trick, though, knowing the secret does not necessarily mean one can pull it off. That is why Holmes seems so mysterious.

Post office on Wigmore Street

Langham Hotel

The Langham Hotel was a large hotel with six hundred rooms, which was built in 1864 at a cost of three hundred thousand pounds. The first of London's grand hotels, it was so prestigious that anyone staying there was automatically considered a gentleman of high standing. Among its regular guests were Toscanini, Arnold Bennet, Frank Harris, Mark Twain, and Napoleon III.

All Souls Church beside the Langham Hotel

Regent Street

The Café Royal, constructed in 1865, was expanded as far as Regent Street in 1870. The basement was a wine cellar and billiard-room, and the ground floor housed a café, luncheon bar, and grill room. The floor above had private rooms until 1909. It was one of Oscar Wilde's favorite French restaurants.

Great Quadrant of Regent Street (viewed from the south)

Piccadilly Circus

Piccadilly Circus

The neon sign of the Criterion Theatre can be seen at the southeast corner of Piccadilly Circus. Although the Criterion Bar, at which Watson met young Stamford, has already been torn down, its entrance was formerly located about eight metres to the east of this neon sign. From there, the narrow, corridor-like bar ran all the way to Jermyn Street.

Pall Mall

*We had reached Pall Mall as we talked, and were walking
down it from the St. James's end. Sherlock Holmes stopped
at a door some little distance from the Carlton, and,
cautioning me not to speak, he led the way into the hall.*
——————— *The Greek Interpreter* ———————

Mycroft Holmes

The strange name Pall Mall was derived from *paillemaille*, an old French game similar to croquet. The game is said to have been introduced to England during the reign of Charles I. This street was the passageway that led to the *paillemaille* stadium.

Theatre Royal Haymarket

In 1830, the market that was on Haymarket Street was transferred to another location. By Holmes's time, Haymarket Street had become home to various theatres, including Her Majesty's Italian Opera House (demolished in 1893); His Majesty's Theatre, which was built by C. S. Phipps in 1897; and, behind it, the Royal Opera Arcade. On the opposite side of the street was the Theatre Royal Haymarket. The building that was inaugurated in 1721 as a small theatre was rebuilt in 1821 by John Nash just south of the original site. The interior was redecorated in 1905. The Theatre Royal Haymarket was flanked on the left by the Carlton Theatre, designed by Frank T. Verity.

Trafalgar Square

In "The Noble Bachelor," Holmes asked Lestrade sarcastically if he had dragged the basin of Trafalgar Square fountain for the body of Hatty Doran.

Trafalgar Square was laid out by John Nash from 1829 over a period of two decades. Sir Robert Peel, known as the prime minister who enforced the Corn Law, extolled it as "the finest site in Europe." The sculptured lions were created after models made by the famous animal-painter Edwin Henry Landseer and added in 1867.

In image text: OFFICE SUITES / TO BE LET / ROBERT LYNCH & COMPANY / 629 0938 / 353 4222 / bureau de change / VINES / CAMERAS / national / Fly the Tube / Fly the Tube / WINTER SALES / UNDERGROUND

Duke of York's Column
and Waterloo Steps

NO PARKING

*"We shall expect you early to-morrow, and when you
get that signal-book through the little door on the Duke
of York's steps you can put a triumphant Finis to your
record in England."*
————*His Last Bow*————

Whitehall

Whitehall is the street on which the Government offices are located. It can be called the administrative centre for the British Empire.

Before it moved to the banks of the Thames River, the Great Scotland Yard also stood on this street. It is said that the name "Scotland Yard" was given to the London Metropolitan Police Headquarters because the grounds formerly belonged to the King of Scotland. The name still remains today in the street name.

Holmes's elder brother Mycroft was a civil servant in Whitehall. He audited the books in some of the Government departments, but eventually became an essential "central exchange," focusing all the separate advisories from various departments and explaining how each factor would affect the other. Mycroft walked to work every day down this street from his rooms in Pall Mall.

Foreign Office

Turning west onto King Charles Street from Whitehall (which runs on a north-south axis), one finds the Foreign Office in the buildings next to St. James's Park on the north side of the street.

St. James's Park

St. James's Park is situated just to the west of the Government offices of Whitehall. At the top of the stone steps at its northern end is the Duke of York's Column. The town house of the Duke of Holdernesse in "The Priory School" and the German Embassy were close by. At the western end of the park is a square with the Queen Victoria Memorial, to the west of which is Buckingham Palace.

Buckingham Palace

Holmes's years of active practice correspond to the last twenty-four years of Queen Victoria's reign. At one time, Holmes adorned the opposite wall in his sitting-room with a patriotic V. R., done in bullet pocks. In "The Bruce-Partington Plans," the Queen presented him with an emerald tie-pin.

New Scotland Yard
(London Police Headquarters)

"I have been down to see friend Lestrade at the Yard. There may be an occasional want of imaginative intuition down there, but they lead the world for thoroughness and method. I had an idea that we might get on the track of our American friend in their records. Sure enough, I found his chubby face smiling up at me from the Rogues' Portrait Gallery."

——————— The Three Garridebs ———————

When the Grand National Opera House, which was being constructed on the banks of the Thames, ran out of funds, Scotland Yard bought the unfinished building and converted it into their headquarters, New Scotland Yard. Because New Scotland Yard was only completed in 1890, Holmes must have associated with Great Scotland Yard for thirteen years.

Westminster Bridge and Big Ben

"Not a moment is to be lost in getting to Poultney Square." "Let us try to reconstruct the situation," said he, as we drove swiftly past the Houses of Parliament and over Westminster Bridge.
——————— *The Disappearance of Lady Frances Carfax*———————

Charing Cross

The most fascinating traveller who ever set forth from Charing Cross Station was, of course, Irene Adler. Holmes captured Oberstein, the spy, by making use of the Charing Cross Hotel above the station. Lowther Arcade, through which Watson hurried at top speed, was in front of the station, and Charing Cross Hospital, to which Holmes was carried after being assaulted outside the Café Royal, lies to its north. Charing Cross Station has come down through the ages, silently watching all these exciting happenings and more.

Charing Cross Hospital

Charing Cross Hotel and Charing Cross Station

Waterloo Place

Cox & Co., a bank formerly located in Charing Cross, was merged into Lloyds Bank and transferred to this building in Waterloo Place. For this reason, the sign of Cox & Co. is still kept at the entrance. Because it was patronized by the Army, Watson frequently made use of this bank.

In any case, one is led to wonder if the tin dispatch-box that Watson placed for safekeeping in the underground vaults of Cox & Co. is still there untouched. It should be filled to the brim with records of Holmes's cases, including many scandals of the late Victorian era.

Entrance with sign of Cox and Co.

Pub "The Sherlock Holmes"

A mock-up of Holmes's sitting room was exhibited in the Abbey National Building Society offices at the present 221 Baker Street during the Festival of Britain in 1951. This room was later moved to the first floor of the pub "The Sherlock Holmes" on Northumberland Street. There it remains today, still delighting Holmes's fans from all over the globe.

The wax dummy of Holmes, which Colonel Moran shot with his air-gun, Holmes's beloved Stradivarius, the apparatuses he used in his chemical experiments, the gasogene—in this room, a dream becomes a reality.

When I find a man who keeps his cigars in the coal-scuttle, his tobacco in the toe-end of a Persian slipper, and his unanswered correspondence transfixed by a jack-knife into the very centre of his wooden mantelpiece, then I begin to give myself virtuous airs.
——— *The Musgrave Ritual* ———

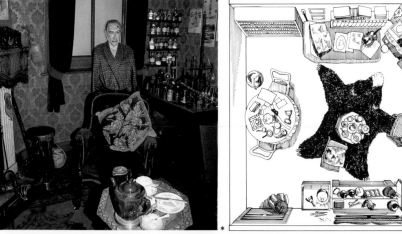

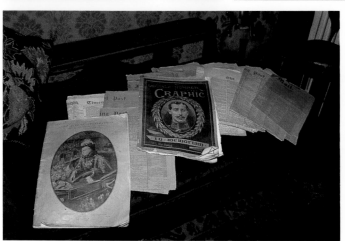

The Strand

Holmes and Watson strolled about Fleet Street and the Strand together for three hours, watching the ever-changing kaleidoscope of life.

Simpson's, which was one of Holmes's favorite restaurants, is in the Strand. He rushed there for something nutritious after fasting to solve a case and also used it as a place for an appointment with Watson.

Simpson's-in-the-Strand

Lyceum Dance Hall
(Lyceum Theatre)

Holmes and Mary Morstan went to meet an unknown man by the third pillar from the left outside the Lyceum Theatre. This was the beautiful theatre before its reconstruction in 1904. Shakespearean drama, with stars such as Henry Irving and Ellen Terry, and plays like *Faust* were exciting the theatre-going public of that era.

Royal Opera House (Covent Garden Theatre)

"Well, Watson, you have one more specimen of the tragic and grotesque to add to your collection. By the way, is it not eight o'clock, and a Wagner night at Covent Garden! If we hurry, we might be in time for the second act."

——————— *The Red Circle* ———————

Covent Garden

It was a bitter night in late December, when the stars were shining coldly in a cloudless sky, that Holmes and Watson visited Breckinridge, a dealer in geese in Covent Garden.

Covent Garden was London's main vegetable, fruit, and flower market. The market was moved to Nine Elms in 1973, and it has been replaced by an arcade with arts-and-crafts shops and coffee shops and by the London Transport Museum. Even so, thirty-odd stalls with clothing, china, and souvenirs enliven the square, and street performers shout out their songs for passers-by, so that the atmosphere of the old Covent Garden still remains.

Bow Street

Passing down the Waterloo Bridge Road we crossed over the river, and dashing up Wellington Street wheeled sharply to the right, and found ourselves in Bow Street. Sherlock Holmes was well known to the Force, and the two constables at the door saluted him.

———— *The Man with the Twisted Lip* ————

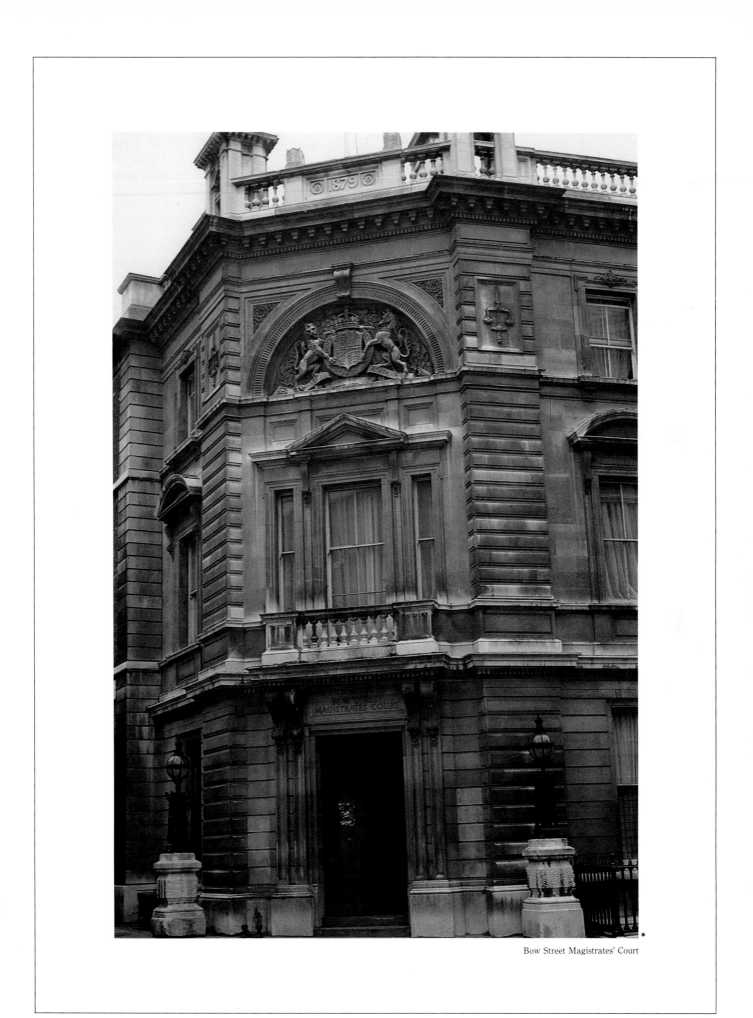

Bow Street Magistrates' Court

Fleet Street

Offices of the Daily Telegraph

Walking east past the Savoy Hotel (founder of Simpson's-in-the-Strand), one finds oneself in Fleet Street, with its newspaper companies and publishing houses. The Daily Telegraph, for example, is at No. 135. Most of the newspaper companies established their offices here after the turn of the century. The offices of the Red-Headed League were located in Pope's Court, off of Fleet Street (to the east of Bell Yard). Fleet Street seems to have been much too wide, however, to have been "choked with red-headed folk" waiting to be interviewed for membership in the League.

Inner Temple

The man that *the* woman, or Irene Adler, married was a lawyer of the Inner Temple named Godfrey Norton. He was quite a handsome man, with dark eyes and dark hair. The Inner Temple, named after the Knights Templars, refers to the association of barristers located within the City. The complex includes a lovely garden, hall, library, dining room, and offices. This quiet corner of London contains ancient buildings straight out of the Middle Ages, contrasting sharply with bustling Fleet Street.

British Museum

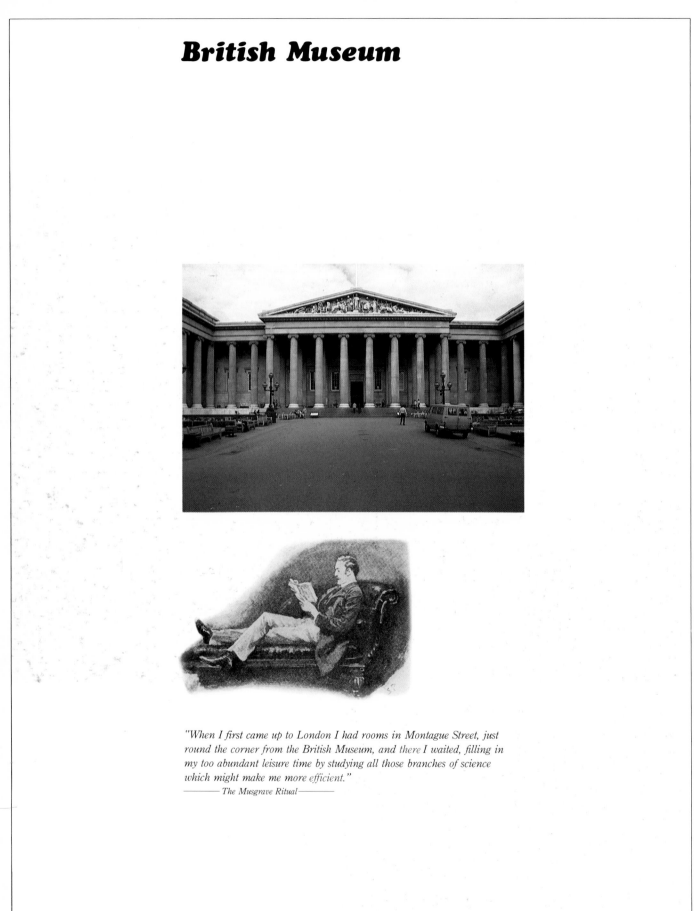

"When I first came up to London I had rooms in Montague Street, just round the corner from the British Museum, and there I waited, filling in my too abundant leisure time by studying all those branches of science which might make me more efficient."
———— *The Musgrave Ritual* ————

The library in the British Museum

The library in the British Museum

Montague Place

Montague Place is the street just to the north of the British Museum, where Violet Hunter, the heroine of "The Copper Beeches," lived. Sir Arthur Conan Doyle also stayed for several months at 23 Montague Place when he first came to London in 1891. To the north is the University of London, where Watson took his degree of Doctor of Medicine in 1878.

University of London

Museum Tavern

At the corner of Great Russell Street, which runs in front of the British Museum, and Museum Street, which leads to Holborn, is the neat little pub now called the Museum Tavern. It was here that Holmes, drinking a glass of beer, asked the owner about his goose-club.

St. Bartholomew's Hospital (Bart's)

St. Bartholomew's Hospital, popularly referred to as Bart's, is the oldest hospital in England. Indeed, almost all the country's famous physicians and surgeons are said to have at one time worked at Bart's. It was in the chemical laboratory of this illustrious institution that Holmes and Watson first met—an appropriate setting for the start of such a famous partnership. Its dignified, elegant appearance, so unlike our image of a hospital, seems not to have changed a bit since that fortuitous meeting a century ago.

Henry VIII gateway

"How are you?" he said cordially, gripping my hand with a strength for which I should hardly have given him credit. "You have been in Afghanistan, I perceive." "How on earth did you know that?"

———— *A Study in Scarlet*————

Bronze memorial plaque

AT THIS PLACE NEW YEARS DAY, 1881
WERE SPOKEN THESE DEATHLESS WORDS

"YOU HAVE BEEN
IN AFGHANISTAN, I PERCEIVE."
BY
MR. SHERLOCK HOLMES
IN GREETING TO
JOHN H. WATSON, M.D.
AT THEIR FIRST MEETING

THE BAKER STREET IRREGULARS ~ 1953
BY THE AMATEUR MENDICANTS AT THE GRUCK GIRL.

Nowadays, Bart's is the Medical College of the University of London. It is known for its Pathological Museum with its 120,000 formalin-preserved human specimens.

Overleaf. By the staircase that leads to the Great Hall are two magnificent murals by William Hogarth, entitled *The Good Christ at the Pool of Samaritan* (left) and *Bethesda* (right).

Paintings by William Hogarth by the Great Hall staircase

River Thames

No fan of Sherlock Holmes can look upon the Thames without remembering the pursuit scene of "The Sign of Four." London Bridge, the oldest bridge in the city of London, is approximately 280 metres long. This wide, abundantly-flowing river is also the stage for "The Man with the Twisted Lip."

St. Paul's Cathedral

When Jabez Wilson saw the square of cardboard with the words "The Red-Headed League is Dissolved," he went searching for Duncan Ross at his supposed new address on King Edward Street. This street runs south from St. Bartholomew's Hospital to just north of St. Paul's Cathedral. If one walks west a short distance from its southern end, one comes upon the Central Criminal Court at the southeastern corner of the intersection of Old Bailey and Newgate Street. The famous Newgate Prison was located at this site until 1902.

Hyde Park and Kensington Gardens

Hyde Park is London's largest park. Among those who enjoyed strolls here were Irene Adler, Holmes, and Watson. The Crystal Palace, mentioned by Grant Munro, was constructed within the park for the Great Exhibition of 1851. It was transferred to Sydenham in 1854, where it was destroyed by fire in 1936.

Crystal Palace

The Royal Albert Hall of Arts and Sciences

The construction of The Royal Albert Hall was originally proposed by Prince Albert, consort to Queen Victoria. It was brought to realization by the Queen in 1871, after the Prince's death. This concert hall has a capacity of 6,500 people. Holmes and Watson went to hear Carina sing there in "The Retired Colourman."

SEARCHING FOR SHERLOCK HOLMES
IN THE WEST END

Without exception, every fan of Sherlock Holmes longs to see Baker Street once before he dies. We decided to fly to London to make this dream a reality.

Once in London, we head first for the Baker Street Underground Station. We speed toward our destination, trying to calm our beating hearts, yet reveling in the excitement of riding on the very Underground that our hero once frequented.

A glance at the plan of the Underground system shows that Baker Street Station is an important center of transportation, where the Circle, Bakerloo, Metropolitan, and Jubilee lines intersect. Few people, though, know that seven blackboard-sized illustrations of scenes from the Sherlock Holmes stories decorate the platform walls of the Jubilee Line. On the platform walls of the Bakerloo Line, moreover, we find decorative tiles with the familiar silhouette of Holmes wearing a deerstalker cap and smoking a calabash pipe, depicted in red and black. Looking closer, we are amazed to discover that the large silhouettes have been made by arranging together thousands of smaller versions of the identical image.

Only two or three other Underground stations, among them Victoria Station with its silhouettes of Queen Victoria and Charing Cross Station with its illustrations of ancient legends, have such wall decorations.

Another pleasant surprise inside Baker Street Station is a pub named Moriarty's. Not only is the name a tribute to the Holmes stories, but much of the interior is devoted to them as well.

In London, the busiest streets are Oxford Street, Regent Street, Tottenham Court Road, New Bond Street, and Baker Street. Throngs of people are seen around Trafalgar Square as well, but, like Leicester Square, this is an open area to which people flock, not a street. The most crowded boulevard of all is Oxford Street. Even on Baker Street, though, at least in the proximity of Marylebone Road, we find ourselves shoulder to shoulder with passersby.

A century ago, the name "Baker Street" referred only to that section to the south of Paddington Street, and the house numbers went only as high as No. 92. The portion of the street to the north was known as York Place.

Accordingly, there are many theories as to the actual location of the 221B Baker Street where Holmes resided a century ago. The present No. 221 is occupied by the offices of the Abbey National Building Society, a modern multistoried structure with not even a trace of Mrs. Hudson's house.

If 221B was simply a fictitious number that Doyle chose at random, then it is still a great mystery exactly where on Baker Street the real building that contained Holmes's rooms was situated. Seventeen steps from the ground floor to the first, a fairly large plane tree in the backyard, across the street from Camden House—there cannot be many houses that fit these conditions. The possible sites that Bernard Davies mentions in his essay "Backyards of Baker Street" (included in *The Seven-*

Photos(p.115~119)／T. Kobayashi and A. Higashiyama

teen Steps to 221B) are the present Nos. 19, 27, 31, 109 and 111 Baker Street. Of these, he says that No. 31 is the strongest candidate and that No. 34 is probably Camden House.

Today, Nos. 19–25 are occupied by JETRO, and No. 27, again, by the Abbey National Building Society. At No. 31 is a gift shop named Avocet, and at No. 34 is the Lindsay Travel Service. No. 109, moreover, is home to the Bristol & West Building Society. Is it fate that seems to keep connecting Holmes to building societies?

Some people may imagine a run-down back street when they hear the name Baker Street. In fact, it is a large thoroughfare, with spacious sidewalks lining a street wide enough for four buses to stand side by side. As we stroll southward on this street, we find the odd numbers on the west side and the even numbers on the east, and the numbers gradually growing smaller. On the left side of the street about a hundred meters past the intersection of Marylebone is No. 108, the back entrance to the Sherlock Holmes Hotel. The front entrance faces onto Chiltern Street, one block to the east.

Just to the south of this back entrance is the Italian restaurant Moriarti. This is the hotel's dining room, positioned so that it opens onto Baker Street. Here, however, the only reminders of Holmes are the silhouettes printed on the menus and coasters; the decor itself has nothing to do with the detective. Inside the hotel, too, is a bar named The Doctor Watson Room.

The Sherlock Holmes Hotel is located on the east side of Baker Street, midway between the first and second intersections to the south of Baker Street Station at Marylebone Road, that is, on the block between Porter Street and Paddington Street. There is a narrow road parallel to Baker Street, running just to its east from the south side of the hotel to Paddington Street, called the Sherlock Mews. Needless to say, it was named after our hero. There is also a Holmes Terrace east of the Waterloo Station.

Walking still farther south, we come across the Baker Street Book Shop at No. 33 on the west side of the street. One shelf is devoted to books dealing with Holmes, but only a few titles are to be found here. Nowhere do we see any evidence of eagerness to provide the customer with all the books currently available on Holmes. Missing too is the nameplate of the Underground train *The Sherlock Holmes*, which, it is said, formerly adorned the interior of this shop.

About 150 meters to the east, at the south end of Baker Street, is the Wallace Collection, which faces south on the north side of Manchester Square.

Leaving our cameras with the guards at the entrance, we enter. There are seven oils by the famous family of French artists, the Vernets, in rooms 8 and 14. The works are by two of the Vernets, Claude-Joseph (1714–89) and his grandson Emile-Jean-Horace (1789–1863). The former excelled in landscapes and seascapes, while the latter was famed for his martial scenes and Arabian motifs. It was the sister of this latter Vernet who was Holmes's grandmother, as Holmes himself related in "The Greek Interpreter." Dr. Verner, who, as told in "The

Buildings reminiscent of the Baker Street of old

Norwood Builder," purchased Watson's practice in Kensington for a high price, was also a member of this clan—thus the reason for the suggestion that it was Holmes who actually financed this transaction unbeknownst to his friend.

The Sherlock Holmes fan is also advised to see the famous portrait of the young Queen Victoria by Thomas Sully (1782–1873) in room No. 1. After all, Holmes was a part of the Victorian era.

Running east from Manchester Square is Bentinck Street, where Moriarty's men tried to kill Holmes in "The Final Problem."

About a hundred meters south of this street, stretching east to west, is Wigmore Street. Here we find the post office where, in *The Sign of Four*, Holmes deduced Watson had gone to send a telegram. The post office is now part of a large building. In answer to our queries, we are told that it was built "when the Westminster was built." As we walk out, we wonder how it could possibly be as old as Westminster Abbey, when, looking up, we see the name of the Westminster Bank to our left. The post office, it seems, is renting a part of the bank building.

Harley Street, which extends south from Regent's Park, is famed for its consulting physicians and specialists. Holmes and Watson came here in "The Blue Carbuncle" and "The Resident Patient," and Dr. Moore Agar in "The Devil's Foot" lived here as well. Queen Anne Street, which intersects this street, is also inhabited by many medical practitioners. Watson had his practice here in 1902. According to C. O. Merriman's *A Tourist Guide to the London of Sherlock Holmes,* Watson's house was No. 9 at the corner of Mansfield Street.

Cavendish Square, with its large trees, is also in the center of a doctors' quarter. This is where Holmes started his adventure of "The Empty House." To its northeast, on Langham Place, stands a magnificent seven-storied building called The Langham, facing north toward Portland Place. It now houses the headquarters of the BBC, but in Holmes's day, this was the ultramodern Langham Hotel. We smile to remember that the King of Bohemia in "A Scandal in Bohemia," Captain Morstan in *The Sign of Four,* and Phillip Green in "The Disappearance of Lady Frances Carfax" all stayed here.

From Langham Place, stretching east, is Mortimer Street. This was the street behind Dr. Watson's house, as mentioned in "The Final Problem."

From Langham Place, Regent Street curves southeast to Piccadilly Circus. It is a large boulevard designed by the architect John Nash in 1813–25 to connect Carlton House in Waterloo Place, residence of the Prince Regent (who was later to become George IV) with Regent's Park, which the Prince had newly acquired. Now, it has become a deluxe shopping area. It was down this street that Holmes and Watson chased after Dr. Mortimer in *The Hound of the Baskervilles.* Paget's illustration depicts it as a narrow road, but in fact, it is quite large, being the main north-south thoroughfare passing through the West End.

Oxford Street, which crosses Regent Street on an east-west axis, was the location of Bradley, the tobacconist, who sold

Regent Street

Holmes's shag tobacco; Latimer's, where Watson bought his boots; the photographer's studio in whose window Holmes found the picture of the murderer of Charles Augustus Milverton; and the Capital and Counties Bank (now incorporated into Lloyds Bank), where Holmes did his banking.

At No. 154 Regent Street, in the window of Lawleys, a store that specializes in deluxe porcelain, we find a bust and full-length figurines of Holmes. According to the store clerk, there are four types of Holmes figurines here, all made by the famous firm Royal Doulton and all very high priced.

The part of Regent Street that curves suddenly before it reaches Piccadilly Circus was called the "Quadrant" by Nash. It was modified in 1923 by Reginald Bloomfield. The Piccadilly Hotel, designed by famous architect Richard Norman Shaw, is on the west side of the Quadrant, while the Café Royal (built in 1865) is on its east side. The Café Royal, despite its name, is not a coffeehouse but an exclusive French restaurant. In "The Illustrious Client," Holmes was attacked in front of the Café Royal, and the criminals escaped by running through the restaurant onto a back street.

Piccadilly Circus—the name brings to mind acrobats and trained horses, but it simply refers to a rotary. Holmes and Watson must have passed through it frequently. At the southeastern corner of Piccadilly Circus is the Criterion Theatre, on the east side of which is the pub Cockney Pride, formerly the Criterion Bar mentioned in *A Study in Scarlet*.

Farther south down Regent Street is Waterloo Place, at the southern end of which is Carlton House Terrace. Standing here is the 38-meter-tall stone column topped by the bronze statue (4.2 meters tall) of Frederick, Duke of York, King George IV's brother, created by Richard Westmacott. The column was designed by Benjamin Wyatt in 1831–34.

The Duke of York is still remembered today, immortalized even in a children's song. He was the second son of George III and served as the supreme commander of the military. It is said that all the officers and men under his command contributed a day's wages to finance the building of this monument.

Formerly, the German Embassy was referred to as the "Duke of York." This was because the embassy used to be located just to the west of this monument.

About thirty steps down a flight of stone stairs to the south of the Duke of York's Column and we are in St. James's Park. This was the place designated for the delivery of the signal-book in "His Last Bow."

At the northeastern corner of the intersection of Waterloo Place and Pall Mall (pronounced *pell mell*) is Lloyds Bank.

Lloyds Bank

> Somewhere in the vaults of the bank of Cox & Co., at Charing Cross, there is a travel-worn and battered tin dispatch-box with my name, John H. Watson, M.D., Late Indian Army, painted upon the lid. It is crammed with papers, nearly all of which are records of cases to illustrate the curious problems which Mr. Sherlock Holmes had at various times to examine.

Site of the Charing Cross Baths

Charing Cross Station

Thus Watson wrote at the beginning of "Thor Bridge" (published in March 1922). In 1923, Cox & Co. was incorporated into Lloyds Bank and moved to its present location. That is why we still see its sign in relief at the top of the entrance to the bank.

One hundred meters east on Pall Mall from Waterloo Place, a turn to the north, and we are on the Haymarket. Another hundred meters to the north, and there is the Haymarket Theatre on the east side of the street. Its actual name is the Theatre Royal Haymarket. It was rebuilt by John Nash in 1820 and was redecorated in 1904. Josiah Amberley in "The Retired Colourman" came to this theatre on the night his wife disappeared.

Still farther east is Trafalgar Square. The street that extends southeast from the square is Northumberland Avenue. Midway down this street on the northern side is what was formerly the Northumberland Hotel, where Sir Henry Baskerville stayed in *The Hound of the Baskervilles*.

To the east of this hotel, we find the pub The Sherlock Holmes. The ground floor is an inexpensive pub that seems to be popular with the young. The first floor has been turned into an elegant restaurant. A part of this floor has been set aside for a reconstruction of Holmes's sitting room, which we can enjoy through a glass partition. The furniture is placed as described in the beginning lines of such stories as "The Musgrave Ritual," "The Priory School," and "The Mazarin Stone." Many photographs related to Holmes, and such curios as the mounted head of the devilish beast of *The House of the Baskervilles* are displayed throughout the ground and first floors.

Behind this pub, at the northwestern corner of Craven Pass and Craven Street, there was formerly a Turkish bath. Holmes and Watson went there in "The Illustrious Client." At the time, it was known as the Charing Cross Baths. According to Mrs. Edie Hardcastle, of The Sherlock Holmes Pub, the underground boiler, the chimney stack, and the doors of the entrance and exit still exist as in Holmes's day.

Craven Street was the site of the Mexborough Private Hotel, where the Stapletons stayed in *The Hound of the Baskservilles*.

Proceeding northeast on Craven Street, we find that it comes to an end at the Strand. The Grand Hotel Buildings, with their curving walls, are on the left corner. To the east lies Charing Cross Station, above which, facing north, still stands the seven-storied Charing Cross Hotel.

In a scene from "The Illustrious Client," Watson was shocked to see a one-legged news-vendor standing between Charing Cross Station and the Grand Hotel displaying a newspaper with the headline "MURDEROUS ATTACK UPON SHERLOCK HOLMES." This was when Holmes was assaulted in front of the aforementioned Café Royal at the instigation of the evil Baron Gruner.

Charing Cross may be considered the center of London, and it is often mentioned in the Holmes stories, among them "A Scandal in Bohemia," "The Man with the Twisted Lip," "The Greek Interpreter," *The Hound of the Baskervilles*, "Wisteria

Lodge," "The Golden Pince-Nez," "The Abbey Grange," "Thor Bridge," and "The Illustrious Client."

The Charing Cross Hotel, which was used by Holmes to set a trap for Hugo Oberstein in "The Bruce Partington Papers," first opened its doors on May 15, 1865. The hotel occupies the upper stories of the northern part of the station.

Across the street from this hotel, at No. 448, was the Charing Cross telegraph office. Currently, the building is owned by Coats & Co., a firm that may be termed a bankers' association. Holmes sent a message from this telegraph office in "The Abbey Grange"; its name appears in "Wisteria Lodge" as well.

The Lowther Arcade, through which Watson raced to get from the Strand to Adelaide Street in "The Final Problem," was located at the front entrance of Coats & Co. At the exit onto Adelaide Street waited Mycroft's cab, which then turned right onto William IV Street, passed in front of Charing Cross Hospital, and returned once more to the Strand. Charing Cross Hospital was where Dr. Mortimer in *The Hound of the Baskervilles* once worked and where Holmes was carried after he was attacked in front of the Café Royal. This building is presently being rebuilt.

Time has caused some of these magnificent stone edifices to become damaged and worn, necessitating their repair or demolition. Only Sherlock Holmes has withstood the elements, surviving untouched for a hundred years.

Corner of the Foreign Office, Whitehall

Charing Cross Hospital under reconstruction

The Strand Magazine, which published the series of the adventures of Sherlock Holmes

Reform of George Newnes, Ltd., publisher of *The Strand Magazine*, at the corner of Southampton Street and the Strand.

HOLMES'S "SUPPORTING CAST"

GASLIGHT

The history of London's gas lamps nearly parallels the history of the city itself during the nineteenth century. Ever since first lit in Pall Mall at the start of the century until forced to give way to the electric lamp in the years between 1886 and 1900, the gas lamp ruled the city nights.

In "The Dying Detective," turning up the gas is used as a signal. In "His Last Bow," this has changed to turning off an electric lamp. Doyle mentions the gas street light only in a few stories like "The Red Circle," "The Red-Headed League," and "The Blue Carbuncle" and uses it surprisingly little as a prop.

THE CARRIAGE

There is an illustration in a children's version of *The Adventures of Sherlock Holmes* that shows Holmes riding in an automobile. An automobile may be bad enough, but one cannot help but shudder at imagining Holmes in something like a jet airplane. With anything but a hansom or a four-wheeler or a landau, the flavour of the Victorian era is lost.

One of the charms of the Sherlock Holmes stories is that one can hear there the clop-clop of horses's hoofs and the screech of the carriage wheels.

In 1891, the carriage fare from Baker Street Station to Charing Cross Station was 16 pence (£2.50 at today's prices).

THE DEERSTALKER

Although the Deerstalker cap, the Inverness cape, and the calabash pipe have become Holmes's trademarks, these are nowhere to be found in the original stories. They are all inventions of people other than Doyle. As we can see in an illustration from "The Hound of the Baskervilles," the headgear that was normally worn on the streets of London was the silk hat. The silk hat first appeared in France around 1780, and full-scale mass production got underway in 1825. Consequently, it is a fairly recent phenomenon. In any case, in Holmes's age, it was the custom to wear something on the head—a bowler or a sports cap, for example. By that time, the export of hats from Great Britain had reached a value of a million pounds (equialent to thirty million pounds at today's prices).

THE PIPE

Holmes, who himself was a devoted pipe smoker, deduced the character of the owner of a certain pipe in "The Yellow Face," stating that "Nothing has more individuality (than pipes), save perhaps watches and bootlaces."

Holmes possessed at least three pipes—a clay pipe blackened from use, a briar, and a cherrywood. The clay pipe was probably for his meditative moods, while the cherrywood was for his disputatious moods.

A man who divides his pipes for meditative and disputatious purposes must have been quite punctilious, fastidious, and argumentative. The calabash pipe had not yet been imported into England in Holmes's day.

THE GASOGENE

The gasogene is an apparatus for making carbonated water. A chemical substance that gives off carbon dioxide is placed in the upper glass bulb, and water is placed in the lower bulb. The carbon dioxide that is produced enters the lower bulb and is dissolved in the water, forming carbonated water. In "A Scandal in Bohemia" and "The Mazarin Stone," Holmes indicated to Watson where the gasogene was, inviting him to help himself. Of course, there would have been a bottle of whisky or brandy nearby, and the result a whisky-and-soda. Holmes himself drank a whisky-and-soda in "The Noble Bachelor" and "The Red-Headed League," but he seems to have preferred a bottle of Tokay or claret.

THE MAGNIFYING LENS

Holmes always carried around a magnifying lens. This might be only a symbol of the great importance he attached to field work. When he went down into the bank's basement in "The Red-Headed League" and, with a magnifying lens, examined the cracks between the stones for a few seconds, for example, he probably was not looking for anything in particular. Mycroft, on the other hand, was an arm-chair detective. He stated that to lie on his face with a lens to his eye was not his métier. Holmes's mastery lay in the fact that he did not rely solely on field work, but on meditation and intuition as well. The late Victorian era was an age when little respect was shown toward instruments, when Scotland Yard (as told in "Shoscombe Old Place") had just begun to realize the value of the microscope.

THE VIOLIN

Holmes purchased a Stradivarius worth at least five hundred guineas (approximately £20,000 at today's prices) at a Jewish broker's in Tottenham Court Road for only fifty-five shillings (about £100 today). A Stradivarius would cost over two hundred thousand pounds today.

Holmes honed his sixth sense with his violin and other forms of music. He is mistakenly thought of as a man in whom reason predominated to the detriment of all else. However, reason alone does not make a good detective. A keen intuition is also necessary, and intuition is fed by a sensibility that has been cultivated through contact with nature and beautiful things. Therefore, the violin plays an important role in Holmes's genius.

THE TRAIN

Holmes appears to have rather liked travelling by train. We often find him casually dashing off to the station.

How did he while away his time on these trips? In "The Boscombe Valley Mystery," he took along a litter of newspapers and spent his time rummaging through and reading them, jotting down notes and falling into meditation. It was also during this journey that Holmes read a pocket version of the poems of Petrarch. He again sank himself into a bundle of newspapers in "Silver Blaze," but also calculated the speed of the train by counting the telegraph posts he saw out the window.

In "The Naval Treaty," Holmes, sunk in profound thought, hardly spoke a word during the entire trip. When a boarding school came into view, however, he suddenly stated his hopes for a better England of the future—a characteristic action.

DOGS

Many dogs appear in the stories of Sherlock Holmes, but few of them are friendly, healthy tail-waggers. The canines in "The Musgrave Ritual," "The Copper Beeches," "The Hound of the Baskervilles," "The Creeping Man," and "Shoscombe Old Place" are beasts that attack men at will. Watson's bull pup, which is mentioned in "A Study in Scarlet," disappeared somewhere when he changed residences. In the same story, a dying terrier is used to test for poison.

Only Toby in "The Sign of Four" and Pompey in "The Missing Three-Quarter" make themselves useful by helping Holmes track someone. Could it be that Doyle disliked man's best friend?

COCAINE

There are some people who look upon Holmes with contempt for having been addicted to cocaine. They, however, are probably unfamiliar with the situation existing in Europe at that time.

In Holmes's day, cocaine had just been introduced to Europe as a tonic. It had not yet, of course, been declared a narcotic, and its pharmacological effects were not well understood. Sigmund Freud, in 1884, was the first to study the pharmacological properties of cocaine by having his friends ingest it and by taking it regularly himself. In 1890, the extract of the coca plant appeared on the market as "a drug that gets rid of the blues" or "a wine for sportsmen." Zola, Ibsen, Stevenson, and Joyce all used cocaine regularly.

CHEMICAL EXPERIMENTS

In "The Sign of Four," Holmes performed chemical experiments with a retort into the wee hours of the morning. In "The Dancing Men," he brewed a particularly malodorous product in a chemical vessel. Chemical experiments are mentioned in a total of seven cases. Holmes even did research on coal-tar derivatives around 1892.

In 1828, German scientists succeeded in synthesizing urea. They also succeeded soon thereafter in separating phenol from coal-tar and in synthesizing aniline. Astounded by German advances in organic chemistry, the English government invited the German chemist Hofmann to England from 1845 to 1863 and established the Royal College of Chemistry in London. The first production of aniline dye by Perkin, one of Hofmann's students, in 1856 and the chemistry boom in England made Holmes a chemistry buff.

Crowborough

Sir Arthur Conan Doyle

House in Crowborough where Doyle lived in his latter years

Sir Arthur Conan Doyle, who through his literary talents made a fictional detective named Sherlock Holmes seem even more alive than any actual human being, spent the latter years of his life in Windlesham in Crowborough. It is located in a hilly area, eighty-three minutes south by train from London Bridge Station and then another ten minutes by car. The building now serves as a home for the elderly.

Crowborough Station

Holmes and Moriarty fighting at the Reichenbach Falls

Postscript

To some day go to London and pursue the footprints of Sherlock Holmes—that is a dream that
many of us, not just those who are Sherlockians,
have long held in our hearts.

Dreams enable us to live rich and vivid lives.
One might even say that man is an animal that
lives by feeding on dreams. We hope that this
brief dream of London we have unveiled on these
pages will serve to foster various hopes and aspi-
rations in many a reader.————The Authors

Profiles of Authors

Tsukasa Kobayashi, M.D., Ph.D.
Psychiatrist, novelist
Prof. of Counseling Institute of Sophia
University, Tokyo
Founder of Japan Sherlock Holmes Club (1977)
Author of 36 books
●

Akane Higashiyama
Writer, translator
Founder of JSHC with husband, Dr. Tsukasa
Kobayashi
Co-author (with Dr. Kobayashi) of 12 books
related to Sherlock Holmes
●●

Masaharu Uemura
Free-lance photographer
Has held several one-man exhibitions
Currently specializing in photography of
American and European architecture

Sherlock Holmes's London

The contemporary photographs were taken by Mr. Masaharu
Uemura, except for those marked with an asterisk at the lower right
corner, which were taken by Dr. Tsukasa Kobayashi and Mrs. Akane
Higashiyama. The photographs on pages 11~33, 52, 89, 97, 111,
112, and 121 were reprinted from *The Queen's London: A Pictorial
and Descriptive Record of the Great Metropolis* and *Round London: An
Album of Pictures from Photographs of the Chief Places of Interest in
and round London* (No. 6 and No. 7 in the bibliography). The
illustrations drawn by Mr. Sidney Paget were reprinted from *The
Strand Magazine*. The captions and essays were written by Dr.
Kobayashi and Mrs. Higashiyama.

Bibliography

1. Baedeker, K.: Lo   nd Its Environs. Karl Baedeker (Leipzig),
   p.586, 1930.
2. Hammer, D.L.: The Game Is Afoot; A Travel Guide to the England
   of Sherlock Holmes. Gaslight Publications (Bloomington, Ind.),
   p.253, 1983.
3. Harrison, M.: The London of Sherlock Holmes. David & Charles
   (Newton Abbot, Devon), p.232, 1972.
4. Harrison, M.: In the Footsteps of Sherlock Holmes. Drake (New
   York), p.292, 1972.
5. Merriman, C.O.: A Tourist Guide to the London of Sherlock
   Holmes. The 'Sherlock Holmes Journal Vol.10, No.1-4,
   1970-1972; and Vol. 11, No.1-2, 1972-1973.
6. The Queen's London: A Pictorial and Descriptive Record of the
   Great Metropolis. (New and revised edition), Cassell & Co.
   (London), p.434, 1899.
7. Round London: An Album of Pictures from Photographs of the
   Chief Places of Interest in and round London. George Newne's
   Ltd. (London), p.300, 1896.
8. Weinreb, B. and Hibbert, C.: The London Encyclopedia. Macmillan
   (London), p.1029, 1983.

●●●

All contemporary photographs were taken especially for
this publication at sites directed by Dr. Kobayashi and
Mrs. Higashiyama.